The Key Facts™ on

Ukraine

Essential Information on Ukraine

By Patrick W. Nee

The Internationalist®

www.internationalist.com

Ukraine is in the midst of a civil conflict. This may or may not affect the core information on this country

The Internationalist®

International Business, Investment, and Travel

Published by:

The Internationalist Publishing Company

96 Walter Street/ Suite 200

Boston, MA 02131, USA

Tel: 617-354-7722

www.internationalist.com

PN@internationalist.com

Table Of Contents

Chapter 1: Background

Ukraine was the center of the first eastern Slavic state, Kyivan Rus, which during the 10th and 11th centuries was the largest and most powerful state in Europe. Weakened by internecine quarrels and Mongol invasions, Kyivan Rus was incorporated into the Grand Duchy of Lithuania and eventually into the Polish-Lithuanian Commonwealth. The cultural and religious legacy of Kyivan Rus laid the foundation for Ukrainian nationalism through subsequent centuries. A new Ukrainian state, the Cossack Hetmanate, was established during the mid-17th century after an uprising against the Poles. Despite continuous Muscovite pressure, the Hetmanate managed to remain autonomous for well over 100 years. During the latter part of the 18th century, most Ukrainian ethnographic territory was absorbed by the Russian Empire. Following the collapse of czarist Russia in 1917, Ukraine was able to achieve a short-lived period of independence (1917-20), but was reconquered and forced to endure a brutal Soviet rule that engineered two forced famines (1921-22 and 1932-33) in which over 8 million died. In World War II, German and Soviet armies were responsible for some 7 to 8 million more deaths. Although final independence for Ukraine was achieved in 1991 with the dissolution of the USSR, democracy and prosperity remained elusive as the legacy of state control and endemic corruption stalled efforts at economic reform, privatization, and civil liberties. A peaceful mass protest "Orange Revolution" in the closing months of 2004 forced the authorities to overturn a rigged presidential election and to allow a new internationally monitored vote that swept into power a reformist slate under Viktor YUSHCHENKO. Subsequent internal squabbles in the YUSHCHENKO camp allowed his rival Viktor YANUKOVYCH to stage a comeback in parliamentary elections and become prime minister in August of 2006. An early legislative election, brought on by a political crisis in the spring of 2007, saw Yuliya TYMOSHENKO, as head of an "Orange" coalition, installed as a new prime minister in December 2007. Viktor YANUKOVUYCH was elected president in a February 2010 run-off election that observers assessed as meeting most international standards. The following month, Ukraine's parliament, the Rada, approved a vote of no-confidence prompting Yuliya TYMOSHENKO to resign from her post as prime minister. In October 2012, Ukraine held Rada elections, widely criticized by Western observers as flawed due to use of government resources to favor ruling party candidates, interference with media access, and harassment of opposition candidates.

Chapter 2: Geography

Location:

> Eastern Europe, bordering the Black Sea, between Poland, Romania, and Moldova in the west and Russia in the east

Geographic coordinates:

> 49 00 N, 32 00 E

Map references:

> Europe

Area:

> total: 603,550 sq km
>
> country comparison to the world: 46
>
> land: 579,330 sq km
>
> water: 24,220 sq km

Area - comparative:

> slightly smaller than Texas

Land boundaries:

> total: 4,566 km
>
> border countries: Belarus 891 km, Hungary 103 km, Moldova 940 km, Poland 428 km, Romania (south) 176 km, Romania (southwest) 362 km, Russia 1,576 km, Slovakia 90 km

Coastline:

> 2,782 km

Maritime claims:

> territorial sea: 12 nm
>
> exclusive economic zone: 200 nm
>
> continental shelf: 200 m or to the depth of exploitation

Climate:

> temperate continental; Mediterranean only on the southern Crimean coast; precipitation disproportionately distributed, highest in west and north, lesser in east and southeast; winters vary from cool along the Black Sea to cold farther inland; summers are warm across the greater part of the country, hot in the south

Terrain:

> most of Ukraine consists of fertile plains (steppes) and plateaus, mountains being found only in the west (the Carpathians), and in the Crimean Peninsula in the extreme south

Elevation extremes:

lowest point: Black Sea 0 m

highest point: Hora Hoverla 2,061 m

Natural resources:

iron ore, coal, manganese, natural gas, oil, salt, sulfur, graphite, titanium, magnesium, kaolin, nickel, mercury, timber, arable land

Land use:

arable land: 53.85%

permanent crops: 1.48%

other: 44.67% (2011)

Irrigated land:

21,750 sq km (2010)

Total renewable water resources:

139.6 cu km (2011)

Freshwater withdrawal (domestic/industrial/agricultural):

total: 19.24 cu km/yr (24%/69%/7%)

per capita: 415.7 cu m/yr (2010)

Natural hazards:

NA

Environment - current issues:

inadequate supplies of potable water; air and water pollution; deforestation; radiation contamination in the northeast from 1986 accident at Chornobyl' Nuclear Power Plant

Environment - international agreements:

party to: Air Pollution, Air Pollution-Nitrogen Oxides, Air Pollution-Sulfur 85, Antarctic-Environmental Protocol, Antarctic-Marine Living Resources, Antarctic Treaty, Biodiversity, Climate Change, Climate Change-Kyoto Protocol, Desertification, Endangered Species, Environmental Modification, Hazardous Wastes, Law of the Sea, Marine Dumping, Ozone Layer Protection, Ship Pollution, Wetlands

signed, but not ratified: Air Pollution-Persistent Organic Pollutants, Air Pollution-Sulfur 94, Air Pollution-Volatile Organic Compounds

Geography - note:

strategic position at the crossroads between Europe and Asia; second-largest country in Europe

Chapter 3: People and Society

Nationality:

noun: Ukrainian(s)

adjective: Ukrainian

Ethnic groups:

Ukrainian 77.8%, Russian 17.3%, Belarusian 0.6%, Moldovan 0.5%, Crimean Tatar 0.5%, Bulgarian 0.4%, Hungarian 0.3%, Romanian 0.3%, Polish 0.3%, Jewish 0.2%, other 1.8% (2001 census)

Languages:

Ukrainian (official) 67%, Russian 24%, other (includes small Romanian-, Polish-, and Hungarian-speaking minorities) 9%

Religions:

Ukrainian Orthodox - Kyiv Patriarchate 50.4%, Ukrainian Orthodox - Moscow Patriarchate 26.1%, Ukrainian Greek Catholic 8%, Ukrainian Autocephalous Orthodox 7.2%, Roman Catholic 2.2%, Protestant 2.2%, Jewish 0.6%, other 3.2% (2006 est.)

Population:

44,573,205 (July 2013 est.)

country comparison to the world: 31

Age structure:

0-14 years: 13.9% (male 3,180,376/female 3,004,250)

15-24 years: 12.1% (male 2,758,374/female 2,645,879)

25-54 years: 45% (male 9,693,346/female 10,355,403)

55-64 years: 13.5% (male 2,573,283/female 3,426,840)

65 years and over: 15.6% (male 2,269,784/female 4,665,670) (2013 est.)

Median age:

total: 40.3 years

male: 37.1 years

female: 43.5 years (2013 est.)

Population growth rate:

-0.63% (2013 est.)

country comparison to the world: 228

Birth rate:

9.52 births/1,000 population (2013 est.)

country comparison to the world: 202

Death rate:

15.75 deaths/1,000 population (2013 est.)

country comparison to the world: 2

Net migration rate:

-0.07 migrant(s)/1,000 population (2013 est.)

country comparison to the world: 113

Urbanization:

urban population: 68.9% of total population (2011)

rate of urbanization: -0.26% annual rate of change (2010-15 est.)

Major cities - population:

KYIV (capital) 2.779 million; Kharkiv 1.455 million; Dnipropetrovsk 1.013 million; Odesa 1.009 million; Donetsk 971,000 (2009)

Sex ratio:

at birth: 1.07 male(s)/female

under 15 years: 1.06 male(s)/female

15-24 years: 1.04 male(s)/female

25-54 years: 0.93 male(s)/female

55-64 years: 0.75 male(s)/female

65 years and over: 0.49 male(s)/female

total population: 0.85 male(s)/female (2013 est.)

Maternal mortality rate:

32 deaths/100,000 live births (2010)

country comparison to the world: 122

Infant mortality rate:

total: 8.24 deaths/1,000 live births

country comparison to the world: 155

male: 10.31 deaths/1,000 live births

female: 6.03 deaths/1,000 live births (2013 est.)

Life expectancy at birth:

> total population: 68.93 years

> country comparison to the world: 158

> male: 63.41 years

> female: 74.8 years (2013 est.)

Total fertility rate:

> 1.29 children born/woman (2013 est.)

> country comparison to the world: 215

Health expenditures:

> 7.3% of GDP (2011)

> country comparison to the world: 77

Physicians density:

> 3.52 physicians/1,000 population (2011)

Hospital bed density:

> 8.7 beds/1,000 population (2009)

Sanitation facility access:

> improved:

>> *urban*: 98.1% of population

>> *rural*: 97.7% of population

>> *total*: 98% of population

> unimproved:

>> *urban*: 1.9% of population

>> *rural*: 2.3% of population

>> *total*: 2% of population (2011 est.)

HIV/AIDS - adult prevalence rate:

> 1.1% (2009 est.)

> country comparison to the world: 52

HIV/AIDS - people living with HIV/AIDS:

> 350,000 (2009 est.)

> country comparison to the world: 26

HIV/AIDS - deaths:

> 24,000 (2009 est.)

> country comparison to the world: 18

Children under the age of 5 years underweight:

0.9% (2002)

country comparison to the world: 66

Education expenditures:

4.9% of GDP (2007)

country comparison to the world: 131

Literacy:

definition: age 15 and over can read and write

total population: 99.7%

male: 99.8%

female: 99.7% (2011 est.)

School life expectancy (primary to tertiary education):

total: 15 years

male: 15 years

female: 15 years (2011)

Unemployment, youth ages 15-24:

total: 17.3%

country comparison to the world: 72

male: 18.1%

female: 16.1% (2012)

Chapter 4: Government and Key Leaders

Government Note:

Ukraine is in the midst of a civil conflict. This may or may not affect the core information on the country's government and leaders.

Country name:

conventional long form: none

conventional short form: Ukraine

local long form: none

local short form: Ukrayina

former: Ukrainian National Republic, Ukrainian State, Ukrainian Soviet Socialist Republic

Government type:

republic

Capital:

name: Kyiv (Kiev)

note: pronounced KAY-yiv

geographic coordinates: 50 26 N, 30 31 E

time difference: UTC+2 (7 hours ahead of Washington, DC during Standard Time)

daylight saving time: +1hr, begins last Sunday in March; ends last Sunday in October

Administrative divisions:

24 provinces (oblasti, singular - oblast'), 1 autonomous republic* (avtonomna respublika), and 2 municipalities (mista, singular - misto) with oblast status**; Cherkasy, Chernihiv, Chernivtsi, Crimea or Avtonomna Respublika Krym* (Simferopol'), Dnipropetrovs'k, Donets'k, Ivano-Frankivs'k, Kharkiv, Kherson, Khmel'nyts'kyy, Kirovohrad, Kyiv**, Kyiv, Luhans'k, L'viv, Mykolayiv, Odesa, Poltava, Rivne, Sevastopol'** , Sumy, Ternopil', Vinnytsya, Volyn' (Luts'k), Zakarpattya (Uzhhorod), Zaporizhzhya, Zhytomyr

note: administrative divisions have the same names as their administrative centers (exceptions have the administrative center name following in parentheses)

Independence:

24 August 1991 (from the Soviet Union); notable earlier dates: ca. 982 (VOLODYMYR I consolidates Kyivan Rus), 1648 (establishment of Cossack Hetmanate)

National holiday:

Independence Day, 24 August (1991); note - 22 January 1918, the day Ukraine first declared its independence (from Soviet Russia) and the day the short-lived Western and Greater (Eastern) Ukrainian republics united (1919), is now celebrated as Unity Day

Constitution:

several previous; latest adopted and ratified 28 June 1996; amended 2004, 2010 (2010)

Legal system:

civil law system; judicial review of legislative acts

International law organization participation:

has not submitted an ICJ jurisdiction declaration; non-party state to the ICCt

Suffrage:

18 years of age; universal

Executive branch:

chief of state: President Viktor YANUKOVYCH (since 25 February 2010)

head of government: Acting Prime Minister Serhiy ARBUZOV (since 28 January 2014); Deputy Prime Ministers Yuriy BOYKO, Kostyantyn HRYSHCHENKO, Oleksandr VILKUL (all since 24 December 2012)

cabinet: Cabinet of Ministers nominated by the president

note: there is also a National Security and Defense Council or NSDC originally created in 1992 as the National Security Council; the NSDC staff is tasked with developing national security policy on domestic and international matters and advising the president; a Presidential Administration helps draft presidential edicts and provides policy support to the president

elections: president elected by popular vote for a five-year term (eligible for a second term); election last held on 17 January 2010 with runoff on 7 February 2010 (next to be held in October 2015)

election results: Viktor YANUKOVYCH elected president; percent of vote - Viktor YANUKOVYCH 48.9%, Yuliya TYMOSHENKO 45.5%, other 5.6%

Legislative branch:

unicameral Supreme Council or Verkhovna Rada (450 seats; 50% of seats allocated on a proportional basis to those parties that gain 5% or more of the national electoral vote and 50% to members elected in single mandate districts; members serve five-year terms)

elections: last held on 28 October 2012 (next to be held fall 2017) election results: percent of vote by party - Party of Regions 30%, Batkivshchyna 25.5%, UDAR 14%, CPU 13.2%, Svoboda 10.4%, other parties 6.9%; seats by party - Party of Regions 185, Batkivshchyna 101, UDAR 40, Svoboda 37, CPU 32, United Center 3, People's Party 2, Radical 1, Union 1, independents 43, vacant 5; composition as of mid-April 2013 - Party of Regions 207, Batkivshchyna 95, UDAR 42, Svoboda 36, CPU 32, independents 32, vacant 6

Judicial branch:

highest court(s): Supreme Court of Ukraine (consists of 95 judges organized into civil, criminal, commercial, and administrative chambers, and a military panel); Constitutional Court (consists of 18 justices)

judge selection and term of office: Supreme Court judges proposed by the Supreme Council of Justice or SCJ (a 20-member independent body of judicial officials and other appointees) and appointed by presidential decree; judges initially appointed for 5 years and, if approved by the SCJ, serve until mandatory retirement at age 65; Constitutional Court justices appointed - 6 each by the president, by the SCU, and by the Verkhovna Rada; justices appointed for 9-year non-renewable terms

subordinate courts: specialized high courts; Courts of Cassation; Courts of Appeal; regional, district, city, and town courts

Political parties and leaders:

Batkivshchyna (All-Ukrainian Union "Fatherland") [Yuliya TYMOSHENKO]
Communist Party of Ukraine or CPU [Petro SYMONENKO]
European Party of Ukraine [Mykola KATERYNCHUK]
Front of Change [Arseniy YATSENYUK]
Our Ukraine [Viktor YUSHCHENKO]
Party of Industrialists and Entrepreneurs [Anatoliy KINAKH]
Party of Regions [Mykola AZAROV, chairman]
Party of the Defenders of the Fatherland [Yuriy KARMAZIN]
People's Movement of Ukraine (Rukh) [Borys TARASYUK]
People's Party [Volodymyr LYTVYN]
Peoples' Self-Defense Party [Oleh NOVIKOV]
Progressive Socialist Party [Natalya VITRENKO]
Radical Party [Oleh LYASHKO]
Reforms and Order Party [Viktor PYNZENYK]
Republican Party Sobor [Anatoliy MATVIYENKO]
Social Democratic Party (United) or SDPU(o) [Yuriy ZAHORODNIY]
Socialist Party of Ukraine or SPU [Oleksandr MOROZ]
Svoboda [Oleh TYAHNYBOK]
Ukraine-Forward! [Natalia KOROLEVSKA]
Ukrainian Democratic Alliance for Reforms or UDAR [Vitaliy KLYCHKO]
Ukrainian People's Party [Yuriy KOSTENKO]
Union [Lev MIRIMSKY]

United Center [Viktor BALOHA]
Viche [Inna BOHOSLOVSKA]

Political pressure groups and leaders:

Committee of Voters of Ukraine [Aleksandr CHERNENKO]
OPORA [Olha AIVAZOVSKA]

International organization participation:

Australia Group, BSEC, CBSS (observer), CD, CE, CEI, CICA (observer), CIS (participating member, has not signed the 1993 CIS charter although it participates in meetings), EAEC (observer), EAPC, EBRD, FAO, GCTU, GUAM, IAEA, IBRD, ICAO, ICC (national committees), ICRM, IDA, IFC, IFRCS, IHO, ILO, IMF, IMO, IMSO, Interpol, IOC, IOM, IPU, ISO, ITU, ITUC (NGOs), LAIA (observer), MIGA, MONUSCO, NAM (observer), NSG, OAS (observer), OIF (observer), OPCW, OSCE, PCA, PFP, SELEC (observer), UN, UNCTAD, UNESCO, UNIDO, UNMIL, UNMISS, UNWTO, UPU, WCO, WFTU (NGOs), WHO, WIPO, WMO, WTO, ZC

Diplomatic representation in the US:

chief of mission: Ambassador Oleksandr MOTSYK (since 24 June 2010)

chancery: 3350 M Street NW, Washington, DC 20007

telephone: [1] (202) 349-2920

FAX: [1] (202) 333-0817

Consulate(s) general: Chicago, New York, San Francisco

Diplomatic representation from the US:

chief of mission: Ambassador Geoffrey R. PYATT (since 30 July 2013)

embassy: 4 Igor Sikorsky Street, 04112 Kyiv

mailing address: 5850 Kyiv Place, Washington, DC 20521-5850

telephone: [380] (44) 521-5000

FAX: [380] (44) 521-5155

Key Leaders:

Pres. (Acting)	Oleksandr TURCHYNOV
Chmn., Rada	Oleksandr TURCHYNOV
Prime Min.	Arseniy YATSENYUK
First Dep. Prime Min.	Vitaliy YAREMA
Dep. Prime Min.	Volodymyr HROYSMAN
Dep. Prime Min.	Oleksandr SYCH
Min. of Agrarian Policy & Food	Ihor SHVAYKA

Min. of the Cabinet of Ministers	Ostap SEMERAK
Min. of Culture	Yevhen NYSHCHUK
Min. of Defense (Acting)	Mykhaylo KOVAL
Min. of Ecology & Natural Resources	Andriy MOKHNYK
Min. of Economic Development & Trade	Pavlo SHEREMETA
Min. of Education & Science	Serhiy KVIT
Min. of Energy & Coal Industry	Yuriy PRODAN
Min. of Finance	Oleksandr SHLAPAK
Min. of Foreign Affairs (Acting)	Andriy DESHCHYTSYA
Min. of Health	Oleh MUSIY
Min. of Industrial Policy	
Min. of Infrastructure	Maksym BURBAK
Min. of Internal Affairs	Arsen AVAKOV
Min. of Justice	Pavlo PETRENKO
Min. of Regional Development, Construction, Housing, & Communal Services	Volodymyr HROYSMAN
Min. of Social Policy	Lyudmyla DENYSOVA
Min. of Youth & Sport	Dmytro BULATOV
Head, Presidential Admin. (Acting)	Serhiy PASHYNSKYY
Chmn., Foreign Intelligence Service of Ukraine	Viktor HVOZD
Chmn., Security Service of Ukraine	Valentyn NALYVAYCHENKO
Sec., National Security & Defense Council	Andriy PARUBIY
Prosecutor Gen. (Acting)	Oleh MAKHNITSKYY
Chmn., National Bank of Ukraine	Stepan KUBIV
Ambassador to the US	Oleksandr MOTSYK
Permanent Representative to the UN, New York	Yuriy SERHEYEV

Flag description:

two equal horizontal bands of azure (top) and golden yellow represent grain fields under a blue sky

National symbol(s):

trident (tryzub)

National anthem:

name: ""Shche ne vmerla Ukraina" (Ukraine Has Not Yet Perished)

lyrics/music: Paul CHUBYNSKYI/Mikhail VERBYTSKYI

note: music adopted 1991, lyrics adopted 2003; the song was first performed in 1864 at the Ukraine Theatre in Lviv; the lyrics, originally written in 1862, were revised in 2003

Chapter 5: Economy

Economy - overview:

After Russia, the Ukrainian republic was the most important economic component of the former Soviet Union, producing about four times the output of the next-ranking republic. Its fertile black soil generated more than one-fourth of Soviet agricultural output, and its farms provided substantial quantities of meat, milk, grain, and vegetables to other republics. Likewise, its diversified heavy industry supplied the unique equipment (for example, large diameter pipes) and raw materials to industrial and mining sites (vertical drilling apparatus) in other regions of the former USSR. Shortly after independence in August 1991, the Ukrainian Government liberalized most prices and erected a legal framework for privatization, but widespread resistance to reform within the government and the legislature soon stalled reform efforts and led to some backtracking. Output by 1999 had fallen to less than 40% of the 1991 level. Ukraine's dependence on Russia for energy supplies and the lack of significant structural reform have made the Ukrainian economy vulnerable to external shocks. Ukraine depends on imports to meet about three-fourths of its annual oil and natural gas requirements and 100% of its nuclear fuel needs. After a two-week dispute that saw gas supplies cutoff to Europe, Ukraine agreed to 10-year gas supply and transit contracts with Russia in January 2009 that brought gas prices to "world" levels. The strict terms of the contracts have further hobbled Ukraine's cash-strapped state gas company, Naftohaz. Outside institutions - particularly the IMF - have encouraged Ukraine to quicken the pace and scope of reforms to foster economic growth. Ukrainian Government officials eliminated most tax and customs privileges in a March 2005 budget law, bringing more economic activity out of Ukraine's large shadow economy, but more improvements are needed, including fighting corruption, developing capital markets, and improving the legislative framework. Ukraine's economy was buoyant despite political turmoil between the prime minister and president until mid-2008. Real GDP growth exceeded 7% in 2006-07, fueled by high global prices for steel - Ukraine's top export - and by strong domestic consumption, spurred by rising pensions and wages. A drop in steel prices and Ukraine's exposure to the global financial crisis due to aggressive foreign borrowing lowered growth in 2008. Ukraine reached an agreement with the IMF for a $16.4 billion Stand-By Arrangement in November 2008 to deal with the economic crisis, but the program quickly stalled due to the Ukrainian Government's lack of progress in implementing reforms. The economy contracted nearly 15% in 2009, among the worst economic performances in the world. In April 2010, Ukraine negotiated a price discount on Russian gas imports in exchange for extending Russia's lease on its naval base in Crimea. In August 2010, Ukraine, under the YANUKOVYCH Administration, reached a new agreement with the IMF for a $15.1 billion Stand-By Agreement. Economic growth resumed in 2010 and 2011, buoyed by exports. After initial disbursements, the IMF program stalled in early 2011 due to the Ukrainian Government's lack of progress in implementing key gas sector reforms, namely gas tariff increases. Economic growth slowed in the second half of 2012 with Ukraine finishing the year in technical recession following two consecutive quarters of negative growth.

GDP (purchasing power parity):

$331.6 billion (2012 est.)

country comparison to the world: 40

$331.1 billion (2011 est.)

$314.8 billion (2010 est.)

note: data are in 2012 US dollars

GDP (official exchange rate):

$173.9 billion (2012 est.)

GDP - real growth rate:

0.2% (2012 est.)v

5.2% (2011 est.)

4.1% (2010 est.))

GDP - per capita (PPP):

$7,300 (2012 est.)

country comparison to the world: 137

$7,300 (2011 est.)

$6,900 (2010 est.)

note: data are in 2011 US dollars

GDP - composition by sector:

agriculture: 9.5%

industry: 31.4%

services: 59.1% (2012 est.)

Labor force:

22.11 million (2012 est.)

country comparison to the world: 31

Labor force - by occupation:

agriculture: 5.6%

industry: 26%

services: 68.4%

Unemployment rate:

7.5% (2012 est.)

country comparison to the world: 82

7.9% (2011 est.)

Population below poverty line:

24.1% (2010)

Budget:

revenues: $55.74 billion

expenditures: $63.37 billion (2012 est.)

note: this is the planned, consolidated budget (2012 est.)

Taxes and other revenues:

32.1% of GDP (2012 est.)

country comparison to the world: 85

Budget surplus (+) or deficit (-):

-4.4% of GDP (2012 est.)

country comparison to the world: 154

Public debt:

36.6% of GDP (2012 est.)

country comparison to the world: 99

36.3% of GDP (2011 est.)

note: the total public debt of $64.5 billion consists of: domestic public debt ($23.8 billion); external public debt ($26.1 billion); and sovereign guarantees ($14.6 billion)

Inflation rate (consumer prices):

0.6% (2012 est.)

country comparison to the world: 10

8% (2011 est.)

Central bank discount rate:

7.5% (31 January 2012 est.)

country comparison to the world: 19

11.97% (31 December 2010 est.)

Commercial bank prime lending rate:

18.39% (31 December 2012 est.)

country comparison to the world: 36

15.95% (31 December 2011 est.)

Stock of narrow money:

$40.44 billion (31 December 2012 est.)

country comparison to the world: 53

$38.93 billion (31 December 2011 est.)

Stock of broad money:

$97.4 billion (31 December 2012 est.)

country comparison to the world: 55

$85.33 billion (31 December 2011 est.)

Stock of domestic credit:

$129.6 billion (31 December 2012 est.)

country comparison to the world: 48

$121 billion (31 December 2011 est.)

Current account balance:

$-14.32 billion (2012 est.)

country comparison to the world: 179

$-10.25 billion (2011 est.)

Exports:

$70.24 billion (2012 est.)

country comparison to the world: 51

$69.42 billion (2011 est.)

Exports - commodities:

ferrous and nonferrous metals, fuel and petroleum products, chemicals, machinery and transport equipment, food products

Exports - partners:

Russia 25.6%, Turkey 5.4%, Egypt 4.2% (2012)

Imports:

$89.71 billion (2012 est.)

country comparison to the world: 36

$85.67 billion (2011 est.)

Imports - commodities:

energy, machinery and equipment, chemicals

Imports - partners:

Russia 32.4%, China 9.3%, Germany 8%, Belarus 6%, Poland 4.2% (2012)

Reserves of foreign exchange and gold:

$24.55 billion (31 December 2012 est.)

country comparison to the world: 56

$31.79 billion (31 December 2011 est.)

Debt - external:

$136.5 billion (31 December 2012 est.)

country comparison to the world: 35

$134.5 billion (31 December 2011 est.)

Exchange rates:

hryvnia (UAH) per US dollar -

7.991 (2012 est.)
7.9676 (2011 est.)
7.9356 (2010 est.)
7.7912 (2009)
4.9523 (2008)

Fiscal year:

calendar year

Chapter 6: Energy

Electricity - production:

    198.1 billion kWh (2012 est.)

    country comparison to the world: 22

Electricity - consumption:

    175.3 billion kWh (2012 est.)

    country comparison to the world: 21

Electricity - exports:

    3.852 billion kWh (2012 est.)

    country comparison to the world: 32

Electricity - imports:

    1.909 billion kWh (2010 est.)

    country comparison to the world: 54

Electricity - installed generating capacity:

    54.88 million kW (2010 est.)

    country comparison to the world: 18

Electricity - from fossil fuels:

    64.1% of total installed capacity (2010 est.)

    country comparison to the world: 124

Electricity - from nuclear fuels:

    25.2% of total installed capacity (2010 est.)

    country comparison to the world: 3

Electricity - from hydroelectric plants:

    9.9% of total installed capacity (2010 est.)

    country comparison to the world: 114

Electricity - from other renewable sources:

    0.1% of total installed capacity (2010 est.)

    country comparison to the world: 98

Crude oil - production:

    80,400 bbl/day (2012 est.)

    country comparison to the world: 52

Crude oil - exports:

    0 bbl/day (2010 est.)

    country comparison to the world: 197

Crude oil - imports:

    155,300 bbl/day (2010 est.)

    country comparison to the world: 38

Crude oil - proved reserves:

    395 million bbl (1 January 2013 es)

    country comparison to the world: 53

Refined petroleum products - production:

    262,300 bbl/day (2010 est.)

    country comparison to the world: 49

Refined petroleum products - consumption:

    320,600 bbl/day (2011 est.)

    country comparison to the world: 39

Refined petroleum products - exports:

    80,980 bbl/day (2010 est.)

    country comparison to the world: 50

Refined petroleum products - imports:

    126,500 bbl/day (2010 est.)

    country comparison to the world: 43

Natural gas - production:

    19.8 billion cu m (2011 est.)

    country comparison to the world: 33

Natural gas - consumption:

    56.2 billion cu m (2010 est.)

    country comparison to the world: 15

Natural gas - exports:

    2.6 billion cu m (2010 est.)

    country comparison to the world: 43

Natural gas - imports:

    44.8 billion cu m (2011 est.)

    country comparison to the world: 11

Natural gas - proved reserves:

1.104 trillion cu m (1 January 2013 es)

country comparison to the world: 26

Carbon dioxide emissions from consumption of energy:

304.4 million Mt (2011 est.)

country comparison to the world: 22

Chapter 7: Communications

Telephones - main lines in use:

12.182 million (2012)

country comparison to the world: 19

Telephones - mobile cellular:

59.344 million (2012)

country comparison to the world: 22

Telephone system:

general assessment: Ukraine's telecommunication development plan emphasizes improving domestic trunk lines, international connections, and the mobile-cellular system

domestic: at independence in December 1991, Ukraine inherited a telephone system that was antiquated, inefficient, and in disrepair; more than 3.5 million applications for telephones could not be satisfied; telephone density is rising and the domestic trunk system is being improved; about one-third of Ukraine's networks are digital and a majority of regional centers now have digital switching stations; improvements in local networks and local exchanges continue to lag; the mobile-cellular telephone system's expansion has slowed, largely due to saturation of the market which has reached 125 mobile phones per 100 people

international: country code - 380; 2 new domestic trunk lines are a part of the fiber-optic Trans-Asia-Europe (TAE) system and 3 Ukrainian links have been installed in the fiber-optic Trans-European Lines (TEL) project that connects 18 countries; additional international service is provided by the Italy-Turkey-Ukraine-Russia (ITUR) fiber-optic submarine cable and by an unknown number of earth stations in the Intelsat, Inmarsat, and Intersputnik satellite systems (2010)

Broadcast media:

Ukraine's state-controlled nationwide TV broadcast channel (UT1) and a number of privately owned TV networks provide basic TV coverage; multi-channel cable and satellite TV services are available; Russian television broadcasts have a small audience nationwide, but larger audiences in the eastern and southern regions; Ukraine's radio broadcast market, a mix of independent and state-owned networks, is comprised of some 300 stations (2007)

Internet country code:

.ua

Internet hosts:

2.173 million (2012)

country comparison to the world: 37

Internet users:

7.77 million (2009)

country comparison to the world: 38

Chapter 8: Transnational Issues

Disputes - international:

1997 boundary delimitation treaty with Belarus remains unratified due to unresolved financial claims, stalling demarcation and reducing border security; delimitation of land boundary with Russia is complete with preparations for demarcation underway; the dispute over the boundary between Russia and Ukraine through the Kerch Strait and Sea of Azov remains unresolved despite a December 2003 framework agreement and ongoing expert-level discussions; Moldova and Ukraine operate joint customs posts to monitor transit of people and commodities through Moldova's break-away Transnistria Region, which remains under the auspices of an Organization for Security and Cooperation in Europe-mandated peacekeeping mission comprised of Moldovan, Transnistrian, Russian, and Ukrainian troops; the ICJ ruled largely in favor of Romania in its dispute submitted in 2004 over Ukrainian-administered Zmiyinyy/Serpilor (Snake) Island and Black Sea maritime boundary delimitation; Romania opposes Ukraine's reopening of a navigation canal from the Danube border through Ukraine to the Black Sea

Refugees and internally displaced persons:

Stateless persons: 35,000 (2012); note - citizens of the former USSR who were permanently resident in Ukraine were granted citizenship upon Ukraine's independence in 1991, but some missed this window of opportunity; people arriving after 1991, Crimean Tatars, ethnic Koreans, people with expired Soviet passports, and people with no documents have difficulty acquiring Ukrainian citizenship; following the fall of the Soviet Union in 1989, thousands of Crimean Tatars and their descendants deported from Ukraine under the STALIN regime returned to their homeland, some being stateless and others holding the citizenship of Uzbekistan or other former Soviet republics; a 1998 bilateral agreement between Ukraine and Uzbekistan simplified the process of renouncing Uzbek citizenship and obtaining Ukrainian citizenship

Trafficking in persons:

current situation: Ukraine is a source, transit, and, increasingly, destination country for men, women, and children subjected to forced labor and sex trafficking; Ukrainian victims are sex trafficked within Ukraine as well as in Russia, Poland, Iraq, Spain, Turkey, Cyprus, Seychelles, Portugal, the Czech Republic, Israel, Italy, the United Arab Emirates, Montenegro, UK, and Tunisia; foreigners from Moldova, Uzbekistan, Pakistan, Cameroon, and Azerbaijan are victims of labor trafficking in Ukraine; Ukrainian recruiters most often target Ukrainians from rural areas with limited job prospects by using fraud, coercion, and debt bondage tier rating: Tier 2 Watch List - Ukraine does not fully comply with the minimum standards for the elimination of trafficking; however, it is making significant efforts to do so; the government reduced its anti-trafficking law enforcement efforts in 2012; as a result of the dismantling of the specialized anti-trafficking police unit in 2011, the number of trafficking investigations, prosecutions, and convictions have decreased; fewer victims are identified and the national referral mechanism does not function effectively in many regions, resulting in few victims being granted victim status by the government; the government did not fund any anti-trafficking protection activities in 2012 and continues to rely on international donors to assist victims (2013)

Illicit drugs:

limited cultivation of cannabis and opium poppy, mostly for CIS consumption; some synthetic drug production for export to the West; limited government eradication program; used as transshipment point for opiates and other illicit drugs from Africa, Latin America, and Turkey to Europe and Russia; Ukraine has improved anti-money-laundering controls, resulting in its removal from the Financial Action Task Force's (FATF's) Noncooperative Countries and Territories List in February 2004; Ukraine's anti-money-laundering regime continues to be monitored by FATF

Chapter 9: Transportation

Airports:

> 187 (2013)
>
> country comparison to the world: 31

Airports - with paved runways:

> total: 108
>
> over 3,047 m: 13
>
> 2,438 to 3,047 m: 42
>
> 1,524 to 2,437 m: 22
>
> 914 to 1,523 m: 3
>
> under 914 m: 28 (2012)

Airports - with unpaved runways:

> total: 79
>
> 1,524 to 2,437 m: 5
>
> 914 to 1,523 m: 5
>
> under 914 m: 69 (2013)

Heliports:

> 9 (2012)

Pipelines:

> gas 36,720 km; oil 4,514 km; refined products 4,363 km (2013)

Railways:

> total: 21,619 km
>
> country comparison to the world: 12
>
> broad gauge: 21,619 km 1.524-m gauge (10,242 km electrified) (2012)

Roadways:

> total: 169,694 km
>
> country comparison to the world: 29
>
> paved: 166,095 km (includes 17 km of expressways)
>
> unpaved: 3,599 km (2012)

Waterways:

> 1,672 km (most on Dnieper River) (2012)

country comparison to the world: 47

Merchant marine:

total: 134

country comparison to the world: 43

by type: bulk carrier 3, cargo 98, chemical tanker 1, passenger 6, passenger/cargo 5, petroleum tanker 8, refrigerated cargo 11, specialized tanker 2

registered in other countries: 172 (Belize 6, Cambodia 35, Comoros 10, Cyprus 3, Dominica 1, Georgia 10, Liberia 10, Malta 29, Marshall Islands 1, Moldova 14, Mongolia 1, Panama 8, Russia 12, Saint Kitts and Nevis 8, Saint Vincent and the Grenadines 12, Sierra Leone 5, Slovakia 2, unknown 5) (2010)

Ports and terminals:

Feodosiya (Theodosia), Illichivsk, Mariupol', Mykolayiv, Odesa, Yuzhnyy

Chapter 10: Military

Military branches:

Ground Forces, Naval Forces, Air Forces (2013)

Military service age and obligation:

18-25 years of age for compulsory and voluntary military service; conscript service obligation is

12 months for Army and Air Force, 18 months for Navy (2012)

Manpower available for military service:

males age 16-49: 10,984,394

females age 16-49: 11.26 million (2010 est.)

Manpower fit for military service:

males age 16-49: 6,893,551

females age 16-49: 8,792,504 (2010 est.)

Manpower reaching militarily significant age annually:

male: 246,397

female: 234,916 (2010 est.)

Military expenditures:

2.77% of GDP (2012)

country comparison to the world: 27

2.4% of GDP (2011)

2.77% of GDP (2010)

Map of Ukraine

Other Key Facts™ Titles

All Key Facts™ Titles are Available at www.Amazon.com

THE INTERNATIONALIST®

2013

www.internationalist.com